ccjc

PLANT CELLS
AND LIFE PROCESSES

Barbara A. Somervill

Heinemann
LIBRARY

Chicago, Illinois

www.heinemannraintree.com
Visit our website to find out more information about Heinemann-Raintree books.

To order:
☎ Phone 888-454-2279
▣ Visit www.heinemannraintree.com to browse our catalog and order online.

Edited by Megan Cotugno and Andrew Farrow
Designed by Philippa Jenkins
Original illustrations © Capstone Global Library, Ltd.
Illustrated by KJA-artists.com
Picture research by Hannah Taylor
Production by Alison Parsons
Originated by Capstone Global Library, Ltd.
Printed by Leo Paper Products, Ltd.

14 13 12 11 10
10 9 8 7 6 5 4 3 2 1

Library of Congress Cataloging-in-Publication Data
Somervill, Barbara A.
  Plant cells and life processes / Barbara A. Somervill.
-- 1st ed.
    p. cm. -- (Investigating cells)
  Includes bibliographical references and index.
  ISBN 978-1-4329-3878-9 (hc)
  1. Plant cells and tissues. 2. Plant physiology. I.
Title. II. Series: Investigating cells.
  QK725.S66 2010
  571.6'2--dc22
                              2009049973

Acknowledgments
The author and publishers are grateful to the following for permission to reproduce copyright material: ©Alamy Images pp. 8 (© All Canada Photos), 31 (©UrbanZone), 40 (©Richard Wong/ www.rwongphoto.com), 43 bottom (©Nigel Cattlin); ©Capstone Global Library, Ltd.: 39 (Peter Evans); ©Corbis pp. 5 (Bettmann), 7 (Clouds Hill Imaging Ltd./David Spears), 36 (Dennis Kunkel Microscopy, Inc./ Visuals Unlimited); ©istockphoto pp. 10 (©Pauline S Mills), 11 (©David Thyberg), 20 (©Vickie Sichaul), 32 (©Elizabeth Shoemaker); ©Photolibrary pp. 4 (Mark & Audrey Gibson), 14 (Ingram Publishing), 15 (Robin Smith), 16 (Mirko Zanni), 17 (Ted Mead), 23 (Johner), 24 (Eisenhut & Mayer), 29 (Joerg Hauke), 37 (Science Foto); ©Science Photo Library pp. 21 (NASA), 27 (David Mack), 30 (Nigel Cattlin), 35 (Steve Gschmeissner), 41 (K Jayaram), 43 top (Phillipe Plailly/Eurelios); ©shutterstock p. 22 (©Olegusk).

Cover photograph of a plant leaf cell reproduced with the permission of Getty Images (Visuals Unlimited/Dr. Martha Powell).

We would like to thank Dr. William Hamilton for his invaluable help in the preparation of this book.

Every effort has been made to contact copyright holders of any material reproduced in this book. Any omissions will be rectified in subsequent printings if notice is given to the publisher.

Contents

Some words are printed in bold, **like this**. You can find out
what they mean by looking in the glossary.

What Is a Plant Cell?

There are at least 260,000 plant **species** on Earth. A species is a group of living things of the same type. Plants range from tiny mosses to giant sequoias. They thrive in deserts, on mountains, and on other plants and animals. They float on the ocean's surface.

But all plants, regardless of size, have one thing in common. They consist of cells. Cells are the basic units of life. The smallest plants have only one cell. Giant sequoias have trillions of cells. Plant cells form roots, stems, and leaves.

Giant sequoias such as these have trillions of microscopic plant cells.

Plant tissues

Plant cells produce three types of **tissues**, which are groups of cells that function together to form structures:

- Ground tissue performs **photosynthesis**, which makes food in leaves. Ground tissue also stores starches and supports plant stems.

- **Vascular** tissue carries water and **nutrients** (substances that help growth and health) through roots, stems, and leaves. Vascular tissue is like the veins and arteries that carry blood in humans.

- **Dermal** tissue is like skin. It covers leaves and stems and protects plants from invaders. Dermal tissue lets sunlight and carbon dioxide into leaves through small holes, or **pores**. Pores in plant dermal tissue also release **water vapor** (water in gas form), oxygen, and other waste out into the air.

Scientist Spotlight

Robert Hooke

Robert Hooke (1635–1703) was one of England's greatest scientists. His natural curiosity led him to study everything from plants to rocks to stars to geology.

His best-known contribution may have been his book *Micrographia* (1665). In this book, Hooke drew accurate illustrations of **organisms** (living things) and tissues of organisms that he saw through a microscope. Hooke described his view of thin slices of cork in *Micrographia*: "The pores of it were not regular . . . these pores, or cells . . . were indeed the first *microscopical* pores I ever saw." Hooke had discovered plant cells, and we have called these units "cells" since then.

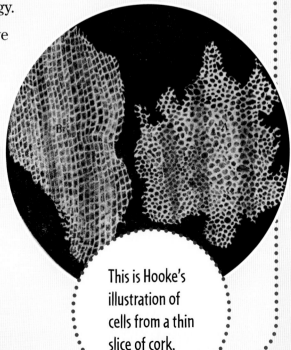

This is Hooke's illustration of cells from a thin slice of cork.

All plant parts have the same basic cell structure.

flower

stem

leaves

roots

Where do life processes begin?

A seed is planted, and its **life processes** begin. The seed absorbs water and nutrients, which allow the seed to develop into a fully grown plant. At first, the seed sends roots into the soil, and a shoot springs up above the ground. As the plant grows, water and nutrients move through the roots and stems to leaves, flowers, and fruit.

Are plant and animal processes alike?

Eating is a normal life process. Unlike animals, most green plants do not need to find food. They make their own food. They take in carbon dioxide and sunshine, combine it with water, and produce sugars and starches.

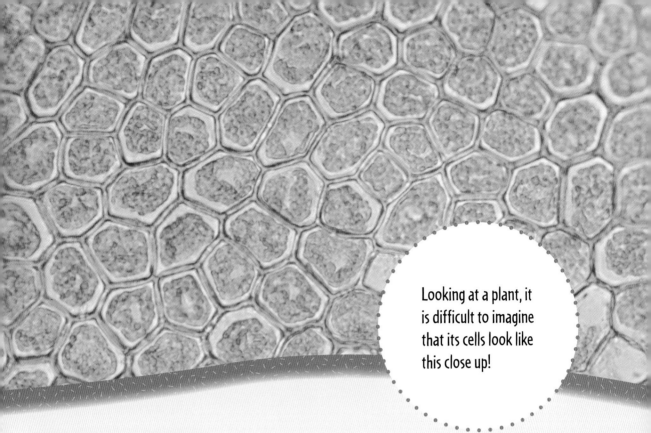

Looking at a plant, it is difficult to imagine that its cells look like this close up!

Plants in motion

To get the most sunlight, plant leaves move to face the Sun. This may not be movement like when you move your arms and legs, but it is movement. The more access to sunlight, the more food a plant can make. That food is turned into energy, which cells use to make seeds. Reproduction is the main goal of all plants and an essential life process.

In addition to sunlight, plants need a good location to grow. They are sensitive to weather. If there is too much or too little water, or if it is too hot or too cold, the plant will not grow well. Weather, soil, and other conditions need to be just right for plants to produce seeds.

Do plants make waste?

Animals make and get rid of waste, and so do plants. Plants produce oxygen, carbon dioxide, chemicals, and water vapor. For a plant, oxygen is waste from making its own food. Plants release the oxygen into the air through tiny pores in their leaves. They also release waste water through the pores as water vapor.

When plants use up energy, they make carbon dioxide. They get rid of extra carbon dioxide like they get rid of water vapor and oxygen.

What Are the Parts of a Plant Cell?

The outside of a plant cell is a **cell wall**. Much like humans have bones to hold up our bodies, plants have cell walls. Cell walls tend to be stiff and rigid, providing the support that holds up all plants, from corn stalks to tall oak trees. Compared to other cell parts, cell walls are thick and strong.

Most plant cells have two layers to their cell walls. Lining the inside of the cell wall is a protective layer called the cell **membrane**, made of **proteins** and **fats** (see page 24 for information on fats). The membrane lets water and **nutrients** into the cell, but it is designed to keep unwanted materials out of the cell.

The bark and trunks of trees are made in part of cellulose, the substance that makes cell walls strong.

Cell walls are made in part from a loosely woven fabric called **cellulose**. Cellulose is full of tiny holes called **pores** so that water and nutrients can flow through the cell walls. You are more familiar with cellulose than you think. The cotton that makes your T-shirt is cellulose. The paper this book is printed on is also cellulose.

How are plant cells alike?

Inside plant cells are rooms, or chambers. Cells with chambers are called eukaryotic cells. Eukaryotic cells exist in humans, animals, green plants, and **fungi (organisms** that reproduce by spores). The cells in soaring redwood trees, lacy ferns, poison ivy, and lemon trees are all eukaryotic cells.

The chambers or structures in eukaryotic cells are called **organelles**. Organelles are tiny organs, much like the heart, lungs, and liver in humans. In plants, organelles do jobs to keep the plant healthy.

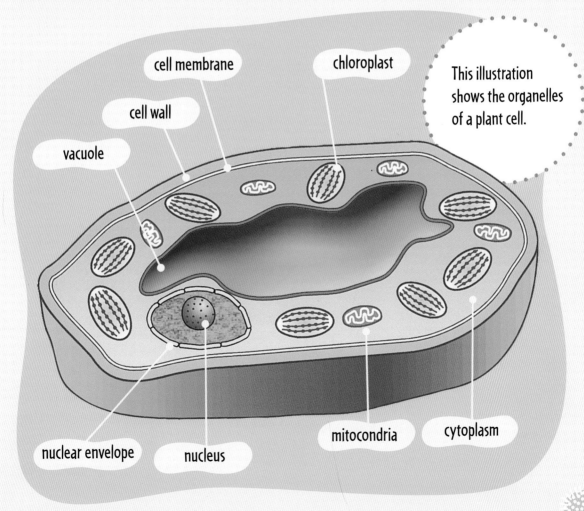

cell membrane

chloroplast

This illustration shows the organelles of a plant cell.

cell wall

vacuole

nuclear envelope

nucleus

mitocondria

cytoplasm

The nucleus

Most organelles in plant cells are similar to organelles in animal cells. The **nucleus** is the control center of a plant cell. It works like a brain does in humans.

Deoxyribonucleic acid (DNA) is found in the nucleus. DNA is the **genetic** (relating to what carries a plant or animal's characteristics) material that determines all the characteristics of a plant. The information in DNA determines if a tree has rough or smooth bark, cones or fruit, and large leaves or needles. It determines a plant's normal height, and if it will have flowers. It even determines how many seeds a plant makes to carry on to another generation of plants.

Surrounding the nucleus is the nuclear envelope, which protects the nucleus. Sticking out from the nucleus is the endoplasmic reticulum (ER). This is a network of tube-shaped structures. The ER arranges chemicals in plant cells into useful forms and carries the chemicals throughout the cells. The ER produces and uses fats and types of proteins.

All plants have the same cell structure.

These oddly shaped baobab trees look as if they were planted upside-down. However, they have the same cellular makeup as other plants, such as daisies.

Central vacuole

Although the nucleus controls a plant cell's activities, it takes up very little space in a cell. Most of a plant cell's space is filled by a storage chamber called a **central vacuole**. A plant's central vacuole is large and important. This is where the cell puts unused food, water, and waste material. Vacuoles hold minerals, such as calcium, sodium, and iron, that the plant uses to live and grow. Vacuoles also provide support and protection for the cells.

Mitochondria

When a plant cell needs energy, the **mitochondria** become active. Mitochondria work as the cell's power center. Mitochondria have their own DNA. Mitochondria get stored food from the central vacuole. They produce energy from the stored food to power the cell's main functions.

Ribosomes

Ribosomes are plant protein factories. Ribosomes help form chains of amino acids, which are compounds made of carbon, oxygen, hydrogen, and nitrogen. These amino acids, in turn, form proteins. The proteins keep plant cells working smoothly.

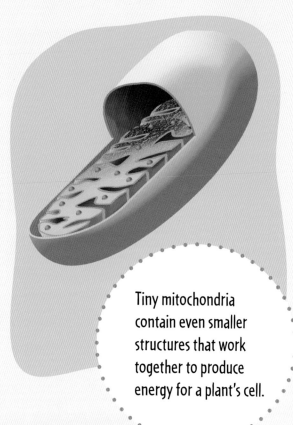

Tiny mitochondria contain even smaller structures that work together to produce energy for a plant's cell.

Science tools: the microscope

Organelles are so small they can only be seen through a very powerful microscope. In 1590 eyeglass makers Zaccharias and Hans Janssen made the first microscope. It was a tube with glass lenses at each end.

Today's microscopes work like the Janssens' microscope, but are much more powerful. They have an upper lens (at the eyepiece) and lenses below. The total magnification equals the power of the eyepiece lens (10x) multiplied by the power of the lower lens (which can be, for example, 4x, 10x, 40x, or 100x). For example, using the 100x lower lens and the 10x eyepiece would magnify an object 1,000 times.

Chloroplasts

Chloroplasts help plants produce their own food. They are green, disklike organs. Chloroplasts contain **chlorophyll**, the green in green plants. **Photosynthesis** takes place inside chloroplasts. Other cell parts that are like chloroplasts store starch or hold the coloring that makes apples red, bananas yellow, and irises a whole range of colors.

Cytoplasm

Any remaining space in a plant cell is filled with cytoplasm, a jellylike substance. Plant organelles float in cytoplasm.

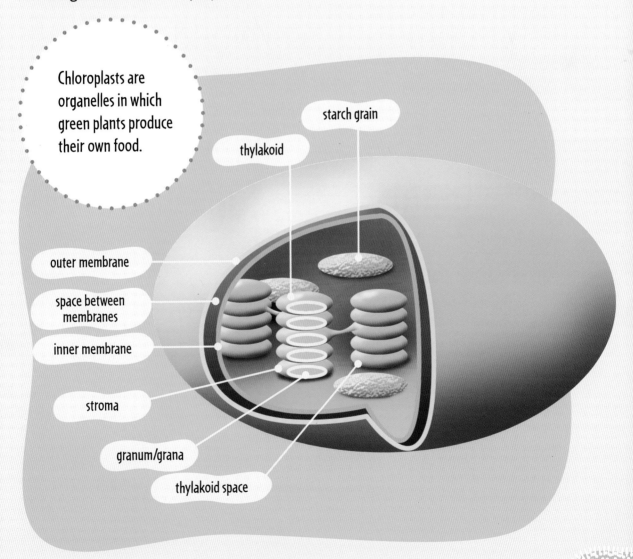

Chloroplasts are organelles in which green plants produce their own food.

starch grain

thylakoid

outer membrane

space between membranes

inner membrane

stroma

granum/grana

thylakoid space

How Do Plant Cells Use Water?

Plants need water, but what kind of water and how much? Plants contain much more water than animals. Fruits and vegetables are made up of 75 percent to 96 percent water, while humans are made up of about 60 percent water on average throughout a lifetime.

Water has several functions in plant cells. Water carries **nutrients** to the cells. **Chloroplasts** in leaves and stems use hydrogen from water to make food. Water fills the **central vacuole**, which helps support a plant's trunk or stem. Without water, plants wilt.

Plants and water

Plants get water through their roots. Too little water, such as during a drought, causes plant cells to shrivel up and die. Thirsty plants do not produce fruit or seeds.

Lack of water causes plant cells to shrivel and die.

Too much water is as bad as too little water. Roots rot in the soil, and young leaves turn brown. Overwatered plants do not produce new growth. Plant cells need to breathe. They take in carbon dioxide during the day and oxygen at night. When there is too much water, the cells cannot take in needed gases, and plants suffocate.

Plants in desert environments

Plants use water in different ways depending on their environment. For example, hundreds of different cacti (cacti means more than one cactus) thrive in hot, dry deserts.

In the desert, a cactus makes do with very little water. When it does rain, cacti cells soak up and store as much water as possible. Their roots get water from the soil. The cactus's skin stretches to hold the extra water. **Dermal** cells on a cactus form a thick, waxy layer. They prevent water from escaping, so the cactus loses very little water through its outer surface. The cactus slowly uses the water, shrinking in size until the next big rain.

These trees could not survive in so much water.

Plants in ocean environments

Giant kelp, a type of seaweed, sway in ocean currents. Kelp, like other seaweeds, live in saltwater seas. Kelp cells do not form **tissues** to carry water, as a tree does. They are surrounded by and take in water directly as it is needed. They have adapted to life in saltwater, which would kill most land plants. They use the minerals in saltwater to survive.

Giant kelp cells use the minerals and salts in saltwater to help them survive.

Rain forests support a great deal of plant and animal life.

Plants in rain forest environments

Deep in the rain forest, hundreds of varieties of fig plants spread their broad leaves toward the patchy sunlight that sifts through the canopy overhead. Figs and other rain forest plants get rained on almost daily. Rain forest plants adapt to getting so much water. It is important to look at the entire rain forest **ecosystem** (organisms and their environment) to see how the plants deal with such heavy rainfall.

In rain forests, rates of **evaporation** (loss of water as a gas) are high, and **water vapor** makes the air sticky with humidity. Some plants get all the water they need from the water vapor in the air. Rain forests have dense plant life, which allows many plants to share the available water. Plants that take in water through their roots quickly move that water through their systems.

They get rid of water through **transpiration**. Transpiration is the process that allows plants to release water vapor through small **pores** in their leaves. Many plants have broad leaves, which allow for high rates of transpiration.

As these examples show, plant cells in different environments take in, use, and get rid of excess water differently.

How Do Plant Cells Make Food?

Plants absorb **nutrients** through their roots. The nutrients are dissolved in water and sucked up through a complex root system. Nutrient-rich water travels from cell to cell, through the stem to leaves, flowers, and fruit. Just as with humans, the better the nutrition they receive, the faster and stronger plants grow.

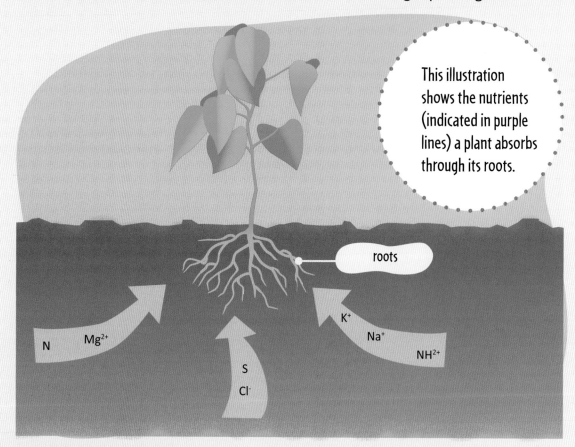

This illustration shows the nutrients (indicated in purple lines) a plant absorbs through its roots.

roots

N Mg^{2+} K^+ Na^+ NH^{2+} S Cl^-

Photosynthesis

Green plants make their own food through a process called **photosynthesis**. Photosynthesis takes place in the leaves of green plants. The process combines three activities. First, the plant "breathes" in carbon dioxide from the air. At the same time, **chlorophyll** in the **chloroplasts** collects sunlight. Water is also sucked up through the roots. Once the main ingredients are present, the chemical process begins.

Photosynthesis is chemistry in action. When the Sun shines, plants remove hydrogen **atoms** (smallest unit) from water (H_2O) **molecules** (atoms bonded together). They also remove carbon atoms from carbon dioxide (CO_2) molecules. Six water molecules combine with six carbon dioxide molecules to make glucose ($C_6H_{12}O_6$). That leaves six molecules of oxygen (O_2) as waste products.

Photosynthesis turns sunlight, water, and carbon dioxide into sugars and starches.

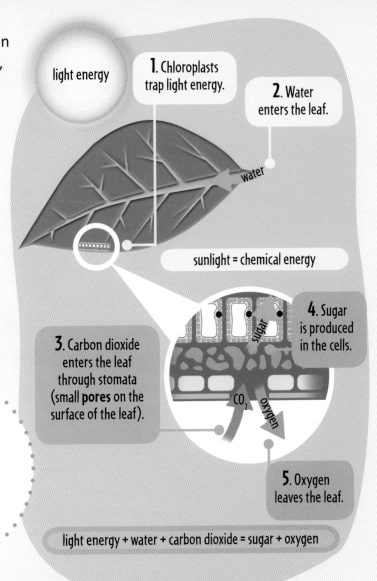

light energy

1. Chloroplasts trap light energy.

2. Water enters the leaf.

water

sunlight = chemical energy

4. Sugar is produced in the cells.

3. Carbon dioxide enters the leaf through stomata (small **pores** on the surface of the leaf).

sugar

CO_2

oxygen

5. Oxygen leaves the leaf.

light energy + water + carbon dioxide = sugar + oxygen

Producing seeds

Glucose provides plants with the energy they need to grow. In the beginning, plant energy is used to produce longer, stronger stems and more leaves. As plants mature, they use energy to produce fruit, seeds, and nuts. In nature, most plants produce seeds.

The number of seeds a plant makes is determined by the plant's **DNA**. Plant cells know to produce a few seeds (for example, coconuts), hundreds of seeds (for example, cucumbers), or thousands of seeds (for example, saguaro cacti). The number of seeds depends on how difficult it is to make new plants. For example, the odds that coconuts will produce new palm trees are fairly high. But the odds that a saguaro cactus will grow from seed to adulthood are very small.

Cells in a Venus flytrap produce enzymes to digest tasty insects.

Poor growing conditions

What happens when there is not enough water or sunlight for photosynthesis to occur? Plants are sensitive to the conditions surrounding them. If there is no sunlight or there are too few nutrients for good health, plants do not produce fruit, vegetables, seeds, or nuts.

Do all plants get food through photosynthesis?

Not all plants live by absorbing nutrients or making their own food. Some plants eat meat. Carnivorous (meat-eating) plants include sundews, pitcher plants, and Venus flytraps. These plants evolved, or developed over time, to eat meat because they grew in poor, sandy soil. The plants needed added nutrients in their diets, and they got these nutrients by eating insects. Meat-eating plants have cells that produce chemical substances, called enzymes, that help plants get useful nutrients from insects.

Meat-eating plants use different methods to trap their prey. Venus flytraps have hairy leaves. When an insect brushes the hairs, cells in the plant react. The plant closes its leaves and digests its dinner. Sundew cells set a trap with shiny glue. Insects step in the glue, and the plant has caught a meal.

A volcanic disaster

When the Mount Tambora volcano in the Dutch East Indies (now part of Indonesia) erupted in 1815, it began a cycle of some of the worst destruction the world has seen. Ash, dust, and gas from the eruption filled the sky. The climate changed, and 1816 became a "year without summer." With reduced sunlight, Earth did not warm as much. In some places, plants did not undergo photosynthesis and produce fruit, vegetables, grains, and seeds. Crops failed, and hundreds of thousands of people and millions of animals died of hunger.

The Mount Tambora volcano prevented sunlight from reaching plants. Their cells did not undergo photosynthesis, and the plants starved to death.

What Do Plant Cells Do With the Food They Make?

Plant cells are always at work. They have one goal: the plant must survive long enough to reproduce. For some plants, such as an apple tree, it may take several years before the tree bears fruit and seeds. For others, like plants on the **tundra**, where the growing season is short, seed production must be quick.

It takes four to five years before an apple tree can produce fruit.

In the meantime, plant cells take in water and **nutrients** and make their own food. The healthier a plant is, the greater chance it has of producing seeds. Although the amount of each **element** (most basic substance) needed for good health changes from plant to plant, all plants need nine main elements. They are calcium, carbon, hydrogen, magnesium, nitrogen, oxygen, phosphorus, potassium, and sulfur. These elements are found in grains, fruit, and vegetables.

What products do plant cells make?

Plant cells use elements to make products they need to support their **life processes**. The products plant cells make are **carbohydrates**, **fats**, **proteins**, and **nucleic acids**. These are the same products produced in animal cells.

Carbohydrates

Carbohydrates are sugars and starches that are the products of **photosynthesis**. They are **molecules** of carbon, hydrogen, and oxygen that provide plants with energy. Sugars and starches are stored in the **central vacuole**. When they are needed, **mitochondria** take the carbohydrates and convert them into energy. **Cellulose**, another carbohydrate, forms woodlike **cell walls** that give plants strength. About one-third of all plant matter is cellulose.

Wheat that we grind into flour is rich in carbohydrates and proteins.

Fats

Plant cells produce fats and waxes from carbon, hydrogen, and oxygen. Fats have more hydrogen and less oxygen than carbohydrates. Many of the oils that humans use in cooking, such as canola oil and olive oil, are plant fats. Plants produce fats because they are excellent energy storage units. When a plant needs to pack a high amount of energy into a small place, such as a seed, it stores the energy in fats. Nuts, such as walnuts and pecans, are seeds with high oil content.

Fats also play a role in protecting a plant's surface from losing too much water. Most cacti and other desert plants have waxy skins. The wax keeps water in and protects the plant from drying out.

Waxes protect aloe vera leaves from losing needed water.

Proteins

Proteins are made from carbon, hydrogen, oxygen, nitrogen, and sometimes sulfur. Proteins help make up cell **membranes**, which are an essential part of a cell. Nutrients and water molecules move into the cell through the membrane. The membrane blocks unwanted materials from moving into cells and lets waste material out of cells. Proteins also control how fast a plant grows and whether it will produce seeds.

Nucleic acids

Nucleic acids are made of **deoxyribonucleic acid (DNA)** and **ribonucleic acid (RNA)**. DNA tells the plant how tall it will be, the shape and color of its leaves, and the type of fruit it will produce. DNA contains thousands of bits of information about the plant. RNA looks for the exact information the cell needs to do its work. RNA copies the needed information and delivers it to the **organelles** that will do the cell's work.

What is in a seed?

Seeds contain hundreds of cells. They have carbohydrates to feed the seeds, fats to store energy, protein for growth, and DNA for characteristics.

If Cells Do Not Grow, How Do Plants Get Bigger?

Cells divide and form more cells. This process is called **mitosis**. In many places, mitosis is most active in spring and summer, when plants grow and produce seeds. In autumn, cell activity slows down. During winter months, many plants lie dormant, or inactive. In tropical and subtropical areas, plants grow throughout the year. Cells reproduce at an impressive rate.

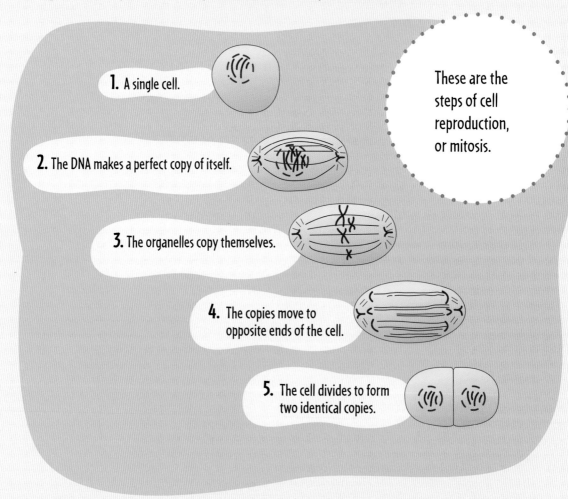

1. A single cell.

These are the steps of cell reproduction, or mitosis.

2. The DNA makes a perfect copy of itself.

3. The organelles copy themselves.

4. The copies move to opposite ends of the cell.

5. The cell divides to form two identical copies.

Cell reproduction uses a lot of energy. Plants need plenty of food to support the growth of new cells. For this reason, young plants put most of their energy into producing leaves. Flowers, fruit, and seeds only appear when a plant is big enough to produce the food—and energy—needed to reproduce.

When DNA is replicated, it makes an exact copy of itself.

When do cells divide?

When conditions are right, cells begin to divide. The first step is for **DNA** to replicate, or produce an exact copy of itself. Each **organelle** within the cell must also divide and reproduce an exact copy of itself. Once there are copies of every organelle, they move to opposite ends of the cell. Then, the cell itself breaks in two. Two identical cells have been formed. From seed to plant death, this process is repeated millions of times.

If you plant a seed and provide the right conditions for growth, mitosis takes over immediately and continues throughout the plant's life. Mitosis provides for growth. It works to replace older, worn-out cells.

How do plants produce seeds?

Meiosis is a special kind of cell division that only occurs in male and female reproductive organs. In meiosis, cells containing half of the **organism's** usual amount of DNA are formed. We call these cells eggs in female systems and sperm in male systems. Each cell has only half the number of needed **chromosomes**. Chromosomes are threadlike structures that carry **genes**, which are the basic unit that carries the characteristics of plants and animals.

This is how meiosis takes place in plants with flowers. The eggs are found inside ovules, which are located in the base of the flower, called the ovary. The pollen, or male reproductive cells, are in the anthers at the end of the stamen. Bees, bugs, and bats visit flowers looking for nectar. They collect pollen and deliver it to other flowers of the same **species**. Pollen may also move from flower to flower with the help of the wind. The pollen moves down a tube into the ovary. The sperm from the pollen **fertilizes** the egg.

The pollen and egg form an embryo (unborn or unhatched offspring). The two halves provide the combined DNA needed to produce seeds.

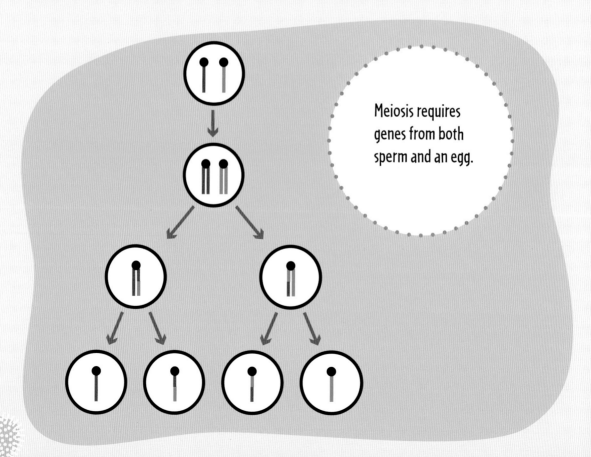

Meiosis requires genes from both sperm and an egg.

These tiny dandelion seeds contain all the DNA in their cells needed to produce new dandelions.

Are all seeds the same?

Seeds consist of many cells. Each cell contains the makeup to create a new plant. It has the products within each cell to support new life. Some seeds have coatings that are hard, like the shell of a coconut, or thin, like the skin of an apple. Some seeds develop inside cones. Other seeds, like those of a dandelion, are tiny, light, and travel on the wind. All seeds, regardless of size or shape, carry the basic DNA within their cells to form a new plant.

Do Plants Get Sick?

When plants get sick, they react differently from animals. As with animals, when plants become very sick, they die.

Sickly plant cells

A plant needs four conditions for it to become sick:

- First, the plant must be the right host (site to take over) for a disease. Some diseases only attack tobacco, while others attack only roses or only cucumber vines, for example.

- Second, the environment must support the disease. It cannot be too hot, cold, dry, or wet.

- Third, a **virus**, **bacterium**, or **fungus** must be on the plant or in the soil.

- Fourth, the disease must have enough time to take over the plant.

This plant suffers from a fungal infection that leaves blotches on the leaf.

Causes of sick plants

Bacteria, fungi, and viruses can make plants sick, just as they make people sick.

There are about 3,500 types of bacteria (one-celled **organism** with no **nucleus**) that make plants sick. Most are found in tropical and subtropical areas.

Fungi (organisms that reproduce by spores) cause blotches or white mildew on plants. They can also cause roots to rot, making plants die from the bottom up.

Viruses (**protein molecules** that cause disease) can be carried to plants by windblown soil, water, worms, or insects. Once in a plant, a virus invades the cells and takes over. Viral infections kill cells, cause yellow areas on leaves, or form swollen lumps on stems or branches.

What other agents make plants sick?

Plants also get sick from insects that can cause damage to trunks, stems, and leaves. When insects bore into a trunk or stem, they cut off the flow of water and **nutrients** through the plant. Leaf-eating insects eat so much leaf material that plants cannot make enough food to keep themselves healthy. Plants infested with insects often starve to death.

Caterpillars cut down on the amount of leaf surface of a plant, limiting the amount of food it can make.

Signs of sickness

Sick plants do not show the same signs of illness as people or animals. They do not moan, shiver, or vomit. Typical signs of a sick plant include shriveled leaves, small fruit, or rot.

Plants may also have blotches, blight, canker, and galls. Blotches are spots on leaves. Blight makes leaves dry up or shrivel. Canker develops a dry, dead section on a plant's stem or a tree's trunk. Galls are large growths on a plant, usually on a stem, branch, or trunk. All of these are signs that plant cells are reacting to disease.

Tomato plant cells protect themselves from attack by producing toxins.

Science tools: centrifuge

Scientists use a special machine called a centrifuge to separate **organelles**. A centrifuge is simply a machine that spins around very fast to create a useful force. When studying cell parts, scientists use a powerful centrifuge to spin cells. The centrifuge moves so fast that the organelles "spin" out of the cells. Scientists can use this machine to help identify viruses affecting plants.

How do plants fight disease?

Cells produce other chemicals to ward off disease. When they are attacked by disease, plants rely on an immune system much like animals do. Cells fight disease in a sort of chemical war. Plants fend off invading insects, for example, by producing **toxins**, or poisons. The toxins are generally **proteins** produced in the plant cells. After one taste, most bugs, birds, and other critters stay away.

When a disease agent attacks a plant, the plant's cells detect the invader. The cells produce a type of protein that fights bacteria, fungi, and viruses. The protein spreads throughout the plant, finds the invader, and destroys it.

Some plants have a third line of defense. They kill cells surrounding the diseased area to stop the disease from spreading. The dead cells form a safety zone that may save the plant.

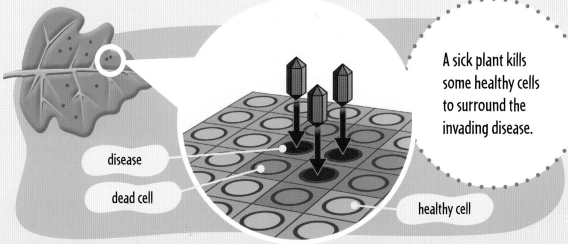

A sick plant kills some healthy cells to surround the invading disease.

disease

dead cell

healthy cell

Are There Really One-Celled Plants?

Breathe in. Breathe out. There is a very good chance that the oxygen you breathed in was the waste from a one-celled (also called unicellular) plant. Billions of one-celled plants float in the ocean, in lakes and ponds, and in rivers and streams. During **photosynthesis**, they expel (release) oxygen.

Most one-celled plants are called **protists**. Scientists break up the protist group into protozoa (animal-like), **algae**, and **fungus**-like protists. Algae refers to a variety of plants, some of which are simple and some of which are complicated. Algae are water dwellers and need sunlight to survive. Like rose bushes and apple trees, algae make their own food through photosynthesis.

One-celled plants form the bottom of the food chain. This means that they feed insects and other small creatures, which in turn feed larger creatures.

One-celled algae

One-celled forms of algae include dinoflagellates, chrysophytes, and diatoms. Algae come in many different colors, from the deep-red of dinoflagellates to the golden yellow of chrysophytes to the browns and greens of seaweed.

Dinoflagellates

Ninety percent of all dinoflagellates are plants that float on the surface of seawater or ocean water. Dinoflagellates have rigid **cell walls** made of **cellulose** and two tail-like parts made of **protein**. The tail-like parts help these red-brown algae move. The plants can produce a poison that kills many sea creatures. Red tides along coastlines are massive clusters of tiny, **toxin**-filled dinoflagellates. Some **species** of dinoflagellates glow in the dark.

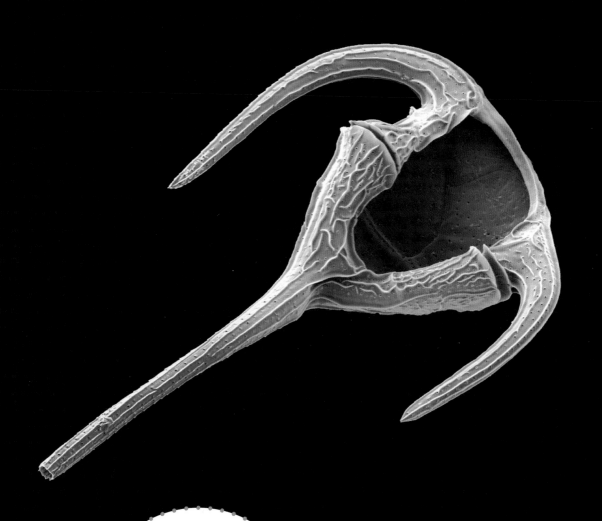

Dinoflagellates are one-celled marine plants that move by flicking their long tails.

Chrysophytes

Some chrysophytes are clear, but most are golden or golden-brown algae. Chrysophytes live in ponds and lakes where water is still and slightly acidic. They are a main food source for tiny freshwater animals. Chrysophytes have rigid cell walls, like dinoflagellates, but they are made stronger with silica, like diatoms (see below).

Chrysophytes get their food through photosynthesis.

Diatoms

Scientists believe that diatoms are the key to life on our planet. The air we breathe is oxygen-rich because these plants float on oceans, lakes, and seas. Diatoms live in ponds and puddles, too. During photosynthesis, **phytoplankton**, which includes diatoms, produce slightly more than half of the oxygen that we breathe every day. Diatoms produce more carbon than the world's rain forests.

Diatoms are considered to be among the best-looking one-celled living things. Their cell walls are made of silica, the same material that makes glass. Diatoms are as delicate as snowflakes and as brittle as a thin glass ornament. They may be round or stringy, and they may live alone or in clusters.

Using dead diatoms

As diatoms die, they sink to the sea or lake floor and collect in the trillions. Diatomaceous earth—dirt filled with diatoms—is the result of these dead one-celled critters. The dirt is used in pool filters, in cleansers, and to get rid of cockroaches. The remains of diatoms might even end up in your toothpaste!

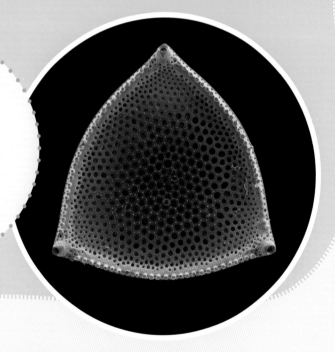

Diatomaceous earth is a collection of trillions of dead diatoms, such as the one seen here.

Euglena

Euglena is a protist that is unique. It is like a one-celled plant. It is also like a one-celled animal. Euglena forms a green scum on the surface of ponds. When sunlight is plentiful, euglena makes its own food through photosynthesis. When it is in the dark, euglena takes in tiny plants and animals, much like microscopic animals.

How Do Plants Get Rid of Waste?

Plants eat, drink, and breathe—just like you, but they have their own ways of doing it. And, like you, they produce waste. Plants do not take in solid food—only gases, water, and **nutrients**. As a result, their waste products are only gases, water in the form of **water vapor**, and waste chemicals.

As plants produce waste, cells store that waste in **central vacuoles**. As water moves in and out of plant cells, it mixes with chemical waste. Plant cells get rid of water vapor and chemical waste through their **pores**.

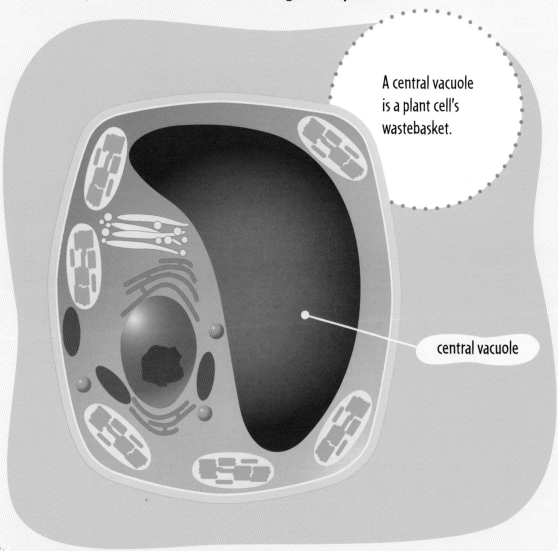

A central vacuole is a plant cell's wastebasket.

central vacuole

Osmosis

Plants rely on a process called osmosis to move water into a root from the soil. Osmosis is the flow of liquids or gases through **membranes**. It allows water to move into and out of plant cells.

Transpiration

Then, water must move up into the leaves. The process of moving water from roots to pass through the leaves is **transpiration**. Think of a plant stem like a straw. The water starts in the soil. Cells that have the least water suck up water through the roots. Water moves from cells that have more water up the plant's stem and into cells in leaves. The water in leaf cells is used in **photosynthesis**, which means that leaf cells always have a need for more water.

Water, water everywhere

Leaves release massive amounts of water vapor. An acre (0.4 hectare) of corn, for example, releases from 11,400 to 15,100 liters (3,000 to 4,000 gallons) of water vapor a day. A large oak tree transpires more than 150,000 liters (40,000 gallons) of water each year.

Water enters the plant through its roots. It is expelled from leaves as water vapor.

Getting rid of waste

In addition to transpiration, plants have other ways to get rid of waste. Some plants actively pass waste chemicals back into the soil. When plants compete for space, they can drop **toxins** into the soil to kill off pushy neighbors.

Another way to get rid of waste is to get rid of the plant parts that store waste. Flowers that grow from bulbs, such as tulips and irises, shed their stalks. The stalks die, getting rid of plant waste and leaving the bulb underground to produce a new flower the next year.

When these autumn leaves fall, they take cell waste products with them.

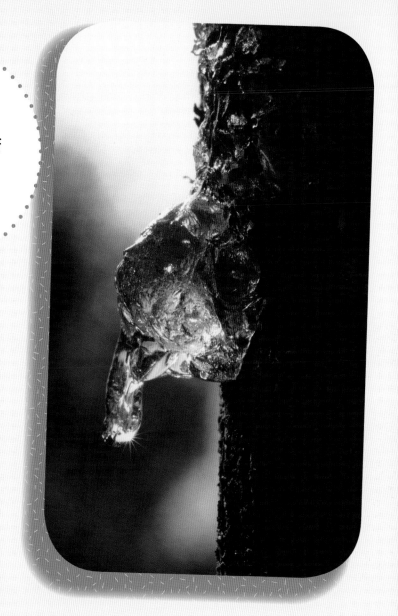

Resin is one way that a tropical tree can rid itself of chemical waste.

Losing leaves and other waste

In the autumn, leaves on **deciduous** trees (trees that shed their leaves) change color and fall off. Trees have absorbed metals, such as lead and cadmium, through their roots. These metals are called heavy metals and are toxic to plants and humans. Plant cells move the metals into vacuoles in the cells of their leaves. The metals, in part, determine the colors of fall leaves.

Tropical trees do not drop their leaves in autumn. They get rid of chemical waste in gums, resins, and saps. Sometimes trees do not get rid of their waste. They store it in cells in the center of the trunk. The waste chemicals cause the wood in the trunk to darken in color. The wood is called ebony or a hard, black wood called heartwood. Ebony and heartwood stop using water and minerals. They serve as storage for some wastes and prevent them from spreading into the rest of the plant.

How Do Scientists Work With Plant Cells?

Ancient Egyptian farmers grew different types of wheat to increase the number of crops. Ancient people in Peru developed more than 3,000 varieties of potato. These cultures used biotechnology to find better ways to grow crops. Biotechnology uses living things as tools.

Here is an example of biotechnology at work. Scientists identify a type of wheat that produces more grain than usual, but that wheat **species** gets disease easily. Scientists also identify wheat that resists disease, but does not make much grain. They work with the two strains of wheat to produce a new wheat that resists disease and yields plenty of grain.

Plant scientists also use crossbreeding to develop new plant species. Crossbreeding mixes characteristics from two varieties of the same species. Crossbreeding lets a scientist mix white roses and red roses to grow pink roses, for example. It helped develop a bigger potato that is perfect for baking, and ears of corn with nice, straight rows of kernels.

Scientist Spotlight
Norman Borlaug

In the 1960s, U.S. food scientist Norman Borlaug (1914–2009) developed short-stalk, high-yield wheat that grows with very little water. For this new wheat, Borlaug won the Nobel Peace Prize in 1970. Since then, Borlaug's wheat has saved more than 225 million people from starvation.

Biotechnology, in this research centre in India, developed cotton plants that grew more cotton!

Think about grapes. People like the fruit but not the seeds. Scientists took grapes with few seeds and crossed them with other grapes with few seeds. Eventually, new grape species produced seedless grapes.

Nature makes these changes often. Scientists have found ways to give nature a hand. The result is more and better varieties of fruits, vegetables, and grains to feed an ever-growing human population.

DNA in the cells of a seedless grape does not send the message for the plant to make seeds.

Glossary

alga (plural: algae) plantlike organism that lives in water

atom smallest unit of an element

bacterium (plural: bacteria) one-celled organism with cell walls but no organized nucleus

carbohydrate sugar or starch

cell wall outer wall of a plant cell

cellulose carbohydrate that provides strength and structure to plants

central vacuole sac or pouch in a cell that stores sugars, water, and waste

chlorophyll green pigment that absorbs sunlight in photosynthesis

chloroplast organelle in plant cells in which photosynthesis takes place

chromosome threadlike structure that carries genes

deciduous tree or shrub that sheds its leaves

deoxyribonucleic acid (DNA) nucleic acid that carries the traits and characteristics of a living thing

dermal skin-like

ecosystem organisms and the environment in which they live

element substance that cannot be broken down into smaller substances

evaporation loss of water into gaseous form

fat greasy or waxy substance produced by cells that stores energy

fertilize cause an egg to develop into an embryo

fungus (plural: fungi) organism that reproduces by spores

gene basic unit that carries characteristics or physical traits of plants or animals

genetic relating to genes

life process one of seven natural activities performed by living things

meiosis type of cell division of eggs or sperm

membrane skin or protective layer

mitochondrion (plural: mitochondria) organelle involved in producing energy

mitosis type of cell division that produces two identical cells

molecule group of atoms bonded together into the smallest unit of a substance

nucleic acid nucleotide that provides directions for cells

nucleus control center of a cell

nutrient substance that helps growth and health in a cell

organelle organized, functioning structure in a cell

organism individual plant, animal, or one-celled life-form

photosynthesis process by which green plants use sunlight, carbon dioxide, and water to make glucose

phytoplankton tiny, free-floating aquatic plant

pore tiny opening or space

protein molecule needed for building and replacing tissues

protist one-celled plant or animal

ribonucleic acid (RNA) nucleic acid in cells that chooses genes and sends messages to cells about what they should do

species group of living beings of the same type

tissue specialized cells in a plant or animal that function together to form structures

toxin poison

transpiration process that releases water from plants as water vapor

tundra large, flat plains of the arctic areas of Europe, Asia, and North America

vascular relating to vessels that carry fluid

virus protein molecule that bonds with cells and causes disease

water vapor gas form of water

Find Out More

Books to read

Cregan, Elizabeth R. C. *Pioneers in Cell Biology*. Mankato, Minn.: Compass Point, 2010.

Dowdy, Penny. *Plant Cells*. New York: Crabtree, 2010.

Fridell, Ron. *Genetic Engineering*. Minneapolis: Lerner, 2006.

Johnson, Lori. *Cell Function and Specialization*. Chicago: Raintree, 2009.

Johnson, Rebecca L. *Powerful Plant Cells*. Minneapolis: Millbrook, 2008.

Lee, Kimberley Fekany. *Cells*. Mankato, Minn.: Compass Point, 2008.

Mullins, Matt. *Super Cool Science Experiments: Cells*. Ann Arbor, Mich.: Cherry Lake, 2010.

Rainis, Kenneth G. *Cell and Microbe Science Fair Projects: Revised and Expanded Using the Scientific Method*. Berkeley Heights, N.J.: Enslow, 2010.

Stille, Darlene R. *Plant Cells: The Building Blocks of Plants*. Mankato, Minn.: Compass Point, 2006.

Websites

"Cell Structure"
www.biology4kids.com/files/cell_main.html
Learn more about cells.

"Plant Cells—The Plot Thickens"
www.eurekascience.com/ICanDoThat/plant_cells.htm
Learn about chloroplasts and the functions of plant cells.

"Plant Science Fair Projects for Kids"
http://homeschooling.gomilpitas.com/explore/botany.htm
For your next science project, why not do something with plant cells?

"Illuminating Photosynthesis"
www.pbs.org/wgbh/nova/methuselah/photosynthesis.html
Discover why photosynthesis is so important to life on Earth.

Become an expert

- Make a model of a plant cell using modeling clay. Add labels for all of the parts.

- Create a poster about algae. Divide the algae by colors or by the habitat (type of place) in which they live.

- Investigate fruits and vegetables that have been genetically engineered. Look on the Internet to find out about advances in corn, potatoes, tomatoes, and other products we eat every day.

- Do a science experiment showing how water moves through a plant. You will need a glass, blue food coloring, water, and a white carnation. In a tall glass, place 118 mL (½ cup) of water and 10 drops of blue food coloring. Make a clean cut on the bottom of the carnation's stem. Place the carnation in the blue water. Record what happens after one hour, three hours, and six hours.

Index